This book belongs to

_____

**I am enough;
I do not have to change
myself to be enough.**

I do not
have to be
perfect
to be loved or
to be accepted.

I can do amazing things.

No one ever made a difference
by being like someone else.

P.T. Barnum

Knowing yourself is the beginning of all wisdom.

Aristotle

I
accept
myself!

It is ok to be proud
of myself and my accomplishments,
I worked hard for them.

I am safe and loved by my
friends and family and
those that know me.

Life will never conform to all of our desires. Ever.

Mark Manson

If you are always trying
to be normal,
you'll never know
how amazing
you can be.
Maya Angelou

"The only person you should try to be better than is the person you were yesterday.

Matty Mullins

I AM SMART AND
OPEN TO LEARNING.

I have the courage to share my true thoughts and feelings.

"Yesterday is history. Tomorrow is a mystery. Today is a gift. That's why we call it 'The Present.'"

Eleanor Roosevelt

"All our dreams can come true,
if we have the courage
to pursue them."

Walt Disney

"It's in every one of us-
to be wise."

John Denver

Now most of all I know that
I am happy to be me.

Take time to pause
and just be.

"You can always, always give something,
even if it is only kindness!"

Anne Frank

She believed
she could do it
so she did!

Don't be the girl
who fell.
Be the girl who
got back up.

Jenette Stanley

Guard your heart
above all else
– Proverbs 4/23

Look up at the stars and not down at your feet.
Try to make sense of what you see,
and wonder about what makes the universe exist.

Be curious.

Stephen Hawking

I am grateful!

Remember who you are!

"You must be the change
you wish to see in the world."
Mahatma Gandhi

Be who you are
and say what you feel, because
those who mind don't matter and
those who matter don't mind.

Dr.Seuss

Your feedback is greatly appreciated!

It's through your feedback, support, and reviews that we're able to create the best books possible and serve more people.

We would be extremely grateful if you could take just a few seconds to leave an honest review of the book on Amazon. Please share your thoughts and feedback for others to see.

To do so, use your phone to click on the QR code, select a star rating, and write a few sentences.

That's it! Thank you so much for your support.

Made in the USA
Monee, IL
20 October 2024

68263665R00048